Praise for

"My Story Your Story His Story"

"My primary focus is family relationships. *My Story Your Story His Story* provides you with an opportunity to have a relational encounter and spiritual influence on your family, for generations to come."

Dr. Gary Smalley, Author of The DNA of Relationships.

"Larry Toller's book, *My Story Your Story His Story*, is an unusually engaging writing that offers far more than casual reading. Unlike most books, Larry offers his readers the opportunity to 'jump into' the story and indeed, become the story. With delightful prose and illuminating style, one feels as if he is sitting on the back porch recounting life's precious memories with an old friend. *My Story Your Story His Story* invites readers to record those things which 'ought' to be recorded for posterity . . . an effort which could produce captured imprints for generations to come!"

Dr. Robert Imhoff, President of Mid-Continent University, Mayfield, Kentucky

"George Mueller, the great pastor and spiritual giant of Bristol, England, studiously recorded what God had done in His life and ministry. His aim was simple: to show the world that God was a 'prayer hearing and prayer answering God.' Countless thousands have been blessed since that time because he took the time to record God's provision. Larry Toller, with wit and insight is giving us all a great look into his life and ministry. Better still, he has given us a tool to challenge us to record our own story, the record of God's dealings in our lives. Take the time to read and be blessed and to write and bless others! Those who follow you will be encouraged to see that God is faithful to ALL generations."

Bill Elliff, Directional Pastor, The Summit Church, North Little Rock, Arkansas

"A simple story is powerful. It can spark the memory, ignite the imagination, and etch truth into the mind. Jesus masterfully used stories to drive home eternal truths to the hearts and minds of his hearers. With simplicity and clarity Larry Toller has recaptured the power of stories. His stories will bring back memories and lessons you may have forgotten. Take time to listen and reflect on his stories; then use them to remember, and learn again from the stories of your life."

Jim Rahtjen, Pastor, Glenfield Baptist Church, Glen Ellyn, IL

"As a child growing up in churches in the rural South, I remember singing, at top of my lungs, the old hymn, 'I Love to Tell the Story.' In this insightful book, Larry Toller helps us to tell that story in fresh ways that will bring hope and encouragement to family and friends. I'm glad that God gifted Larry to offer this book to us."

Dr. Andrew Westmoreland, President, Samford University, Birmingham, Alabama

"What a wonderful gift Larry Toller has given the readers of this special book and journal. With warmth and humor these everyday glimpses of eternity inspire and invite us to recognize those moments in our own lives. As story begets story and memory begets memory I invite you to participate and record your own moments of the heart. You'll be glad you did, and so will those you love."

Nate Adams, Author, Executive Director, Illinois Baptist State Association

---

For more information on *My Story Your Story His Story* and author/speaker Larry Toller, visit: www.memoryjournaling.com

My | Your | His
STORY

A MEMORY JOURNAL

LARRY A. TOLLER

&

YOU

TATE PUBLISHING & *Enterprises*

060821

This book is dedicated:

To those who have gone before us,
whose story will never be told,
because it was never written.

To the main characters in my story:
my wife, my children,
my family and my friends.

To the memory of:
My father, Bill Toller and
my sweet mother-in-law, Cleta Nixon

Acknowledgments

There are so many people who have helped me with this book; I hesitate to mention names for fear of leaving someone out. But I never pay attention to my hesitations.

Thank-you:
To all who proof read over the years, especially April Jagger,
Wes and Sandra Toller and Carole Doom.
To Karen Jordan for her
expert assistance and encouragement.
To Dan Jordan (Karen's husband)
for keeping me humble.
To Governor Mike Huckabee for the
foreword and the friendship.
To Chris Pyle on the Governor's staff for being a true friend
from the beginning of the "great adventure."
To my staff and co-workers at the
Illinois Baptist State Association.
To the wonderful staff of the
Tate Publishing Company.
To my brother, Wes,
my son, Michael and
my daughter-in-law, Paula-Beth,
for use of their songs.

All photos by Larry Toller.
Graphic for "The Light of Christmas"
by Laura Toller

TABLE OF CONTENTS

FOREWORD

Shortly after becoming Arkansas' governor, I had the opportunity to hire my long-time friend, Larry Toller. I'm not sure what it says about his time in the governor's office that he chose not to include any stories from his experience there, but I could submit a few of my own.

Every class has its clown, and I guess every staff does as well. Larry served this role with distinction during the four years he worked for me. It was a rare staff meeting that passed without Larry having some "interesting" anecdote or sage words of advice for the rest of us which we, of course, immediately and wisely ignored.

Larry has always had a knack for recognizing the humor in everyday situations. He's also had a way of recognizing the deeper significance of what might seem like an insignificant event.

Through the stories in these pages, Larry follows the example of Jesus, the greatest communicator who ever lived, by teaching us simple lessons from everyday situations. Jesus taught his disciples, and us, the important lessons by observing life as it happened.

We would never have the benefit of learning the great lessons of Jesus had no one taken the time to write them down. Larry shows us how easy it is to record one's memories (and believe me, if Larry can do it, anyone can), and he gives us simple prompts to get us started. I know of no greater gift a parent or grandparent could give their children and grandchildren than a written record of their passions, joys, fears, loves, beliefs and convictions expressed through "memory journals."

How many of us wish we had just five more minutes of conversation with a mother, father or grandparent? The lessons we learned in those casual conversations were sometimes subtle and sometimes obvious, but they were gained because someone lived the experiences and lived to tell about them.

I hope you enjoy this book but, more importantly, I hope you find that it spurs you to unlock those memories and to record them for posterity. In the process, you'll be creating an everlasting gift for future generations.

Mike Huckabee
Governor of Arkansas

INTRODUCTION

It's all about you.

In the amazing book, The Purpose Driven Life,
Rick Warren begins the first chapter
with the phrase, "It's not about you."

He's right.
From our perspective,
it's all about God.

But from God's perspective,
it's all about me.

He loves me
as if there is no one else to love.

God is the author of my life.
He is a masterful storyteller.

God has wonders for me to observe.

He has jokes and humorous tales
which will create laughter
and joy.

He has emotional stories
which will stir hearts and
cause a tear to fall.

He has amazing adventures,
dramas and mysteries,
which will astound and amaze.

All told through my personal journey
and written on the pages of time.

God reveals Himself and His Truth
so clearly,
so obscurely,
so quickly,
so slowly,
sometimes with a faint whisper,
sometimes with a deafening yell.

As I walk the pathway
in this pilgrimage to know Him,
I must record
His story through my story.

One purpose of this book is to share with you
bits and pieces of my memory and
the lessons learned.

These are brief glimpses,
these are simple stories,
these are profound lessons
written by the

Creator and Sustainer of the universe:
The Author of my life.
He is also the Author of your life.
Yes,

_____

(write your name here)

it's all about you!

Which brings me to the other purpose of this book:
You have a story to tell.
When reading my stories,
you will be reminded of
an experience of your own,
a memory.

You don't have to be a professional writer
to record your experience.
All you need is a pen.
I have provided the paper.

God has allowed you the ability to remember.

Write down your experiences and
lessons learned from God.

After each story,
there are writing prompts to assist you in
processing your memories.

This process is what I call
"Memory Journaling"

You have my permission to
totally ignore these prompts.

My desire is for you to share
His story in you.

You may keep these stories private or
you may, like me,
want to share them.

Then share!

Share them with me!

Share them with family
and friends.

Pass this book we have written together
from generation to generation,
so that God's story in you can be known.

Let's get started!

Hebrews 12:1-3 (NASB)
Therefore, since we have so great a cloud of witnesses surrounding us, let us also lay aside every encumbrance and the sin which so easily entangles us, and let us run with endurance the race that is set before us, fixing our eyes on Jesus, the author and perfecter of faith, who for the joy set before Him endured the cross, despising the shame, and has sat down at the right hand of the throne of God. For consider Him who has endured such hostility by sinners against Himself, so that you will not grow weary and lose heart.

WRITTEN IN RED

As the Youth and Education Minister at the
Harrodsburg Baptist Church in
Harrodsburg, Kentucky, in the mid-seventies,
I was given the responsibility of delivering
announcements to the congregation.

Although it was a boring responsibility,
I tried to liven it up with the Texas humor that
occasionally is admired in Kentucky,
but in most cases elicited only blank expressions.

I thought
the humor would loosen them up and
make them more receptive to God's message or
at least thankful the message had finally come.

Often, after the service I was handed a note from a
retired English teacher.

The note pointed out my grammatical
mistakes for the week.

She once gave me a book on grammar
with a note in the front indicating the pages
I should read first,
written in red.

Throughout the book were markings,
underlines, stars and asterisks,
all written in red.

She really didn't realize how much
of my poor grammar was real and how much
was for her benefit.

(You should have determined by now
it was all real.)

Even though she seemed
somewhat irritated with me,
I think the exchange brought her a little joy.

It was a fun game for me and I think it was for her.
I'm sure Nelva has gone on to be
with the Lord by now.

If she somehow becomes aware of these writings,
I am sure when I enter heaven,
I will be handed a note from Nelva,
written in red ink.

One aspect of this book
which may irritate some is
the centering of every line.

This is my favorite style of writing because it reminds me of the
writing style of one of my heroes: Grady Nutt.
Soon, after getting to heaven,
I guess I will need to apologize to him.

If apologies are to be given in heaven,
I will be busy for a while.

Most of the time will be spent
apologizing to my Lord and Savior.

But before I get started,
He will put His finger to His lips,
say a gentle, "shhh"
and hand me a note,
written in red.

Hebrews 9:22 (NLT)

In fact, we can say that according to the Law of Moses, nearly everything was purified by sprinkling with blood. Without the shedding of blood, there is no forgiveness of sins.

SELAH

Words and Music by Michael Toller

Start of my day
Always the same
Everything seems to be rushed
Where is my time
So hard to find
A simple hush

Selah, Selah, Selah, Selah

End of my day
Sleep depraved
Thankful that my day is through
I pray to the sky
Holding open my eyes
When do I spend time with you

Selah, Selah, Selah, Selah

Be still, Be Quiet
Listen, Reflect
Be still, Be Quiet
Listen, Reflect

Selah, Selah, Selah, Selah

Pause and reflect

YOUR STORY

The Introduction and first story explain why I am writing this book, my preferred style, some of my short-comings, and then I related the story to a spiritual truth.

One of the most neglected words of the Bible is
"Selah."
It means: pause and reflect.
I encourage you as you read these stories,
poems, song lyrics and scriptures,
to pause and reflect.

Then write!

Tell a story explaining why you would like to share your stories and that, in spite of inadequacies, God has a story for you to tell.

_____

_____

_____

_____

_____

_____

_____

_____

BEAUTIFUL WORDS

(My Daughter, Rebekah, was 4.)

How many of you have been separated from your very young
children for more than twenty-four hours?

What happens when you return?

They come running and
throw you on the ground and
hug and kiss you.

I don't have to wait twenty-four hours.
I just come home for lunch;
my daughter comes running.

She jumps into my arms and
we hug and kiss.

I sit down with her in my lap and
she tells me about her day.

She shows me the bruises and hurts
she recently acquired.
Then she updates me on the
healing of those injuries.
I kiss those hurts and make them "all better."

She tells me of her many new experiences.
Anyone else might have difficulty
understanding what she says,
but I understand;
I listen intently.

These are special moments.

But the best moment of all
is when she looks up at me to say,
without prompting,
the beautiful words:
"I love you!"

Your God wants you
to come running to Him and
leap in His lap.
Then, He wants you to tell
Him about your day.

He wants you to show Him the
bruises and hurts
you recently acquired.
He wants to kiss those bruises and
make the hurts go away.

He wants you to tell Him
all of your experiences.
Anyone else would have difficulty

understanding what you say,
but He understands;
He listens intently.

These are special moments.

But more than anything
as He holds you in the safety of His arms,
He desires to hear you say,
without prompting,
the beautiful words:
"I love you!"

Deuteronomy 6:5 (NIV)

*Love the LORD your God with all your heart and all your soul
and with all your strength.*

REBEKAH SKATES

On the ice she must go
Sometimes fast sometimes slow
In figure eight or a spin
Expressing joy from within

Perfect balance and grace
Wind blows across her face
Gliding upon two sharp blades
By the audience parades

In movement so precise
A thin line in the ice
Creating a fleeting art
The cold brings warmth to the heart

Across frozen water
Brings pride to her father
Glistens in reflected light
Continues her graceful flight

LIL SIS
Words and Music by Michael Toller

I was fifteen when you came in my life
I can still hear your infant cries
Learning to dance and learning to sing
You were such a sight to see

Now you are a little girl
Shoved into this messed up world
Trusting with your childlike faith
As I look into your face

I can see your innocence
When I look into your eyes
Then I'll give you a kiss
Hold on to Jesus Christ

One day you will grow
and then I'll be really old
And when I'm turning grey
I hope, I hope and pray

That I will see your innocence
When I look into your eyes
Then I'll give you a kiss
Hold on to Jesus Christ

Hold on to Jesus Christ

Little Sis hold on

Lil Sis © 2006 Michael Toller
Used by permission

YOUR STORY

Relate a story prompted in your memory
by what you have just read.

It doesn't even have to be similar.

What ever the memory, write it down.

Did God reveal a spiritual truth
through the experience you have written?

Two other ways of
"Memory Journaling" are
writing poetry and
music.

You may or may not be a poet or song writer.
Give it a try or write as you wish.

_____

_____

_____

_____

_____

_____

_____

MEMA'S HOUSE

I loved going to Mema and Papaw's house in Olney, Texas.

My maternal grandparents were two of the most loving people
in my life and their house provided only good memories.

On holidays, uncles, aunts and cousins attempted to make it to
West Oak Street to
catch up on each others' lives,
update one another on their latest struggles,
brag on their kids' achievements,
compare sports observations, and
generally enjoy each others' company.

The most important accomplishment
of the day was to enjoy Mema's cooking.

Uncle Leon, Aunt Bernice, Kaye and Kris,
Uncle Dennis, Aunt Margie,
Denny-Ralph and Denise,
my family, great uncles, great aunts,
and second cousins.

33

Fascinating stories were told with great skill by my
Great Uncle Bill who was born in England.
His accent made the stories
even more interesting.
He and Aunt Ruth had no children and
traveled across the country.
They took lots of pictures and
in the evening we traveled with them
vicariously through slide shows.

Everyone had a funny story or
an unbelievable adventure to share.

The football or baseball game would be on the TV.
All the men gathered around.
Statistics and predictions permeated the air.
No one had more information memorized
than Papaw.

In the kitchen,
the women shared stories
or they were being entertained
by one of the children.

Outside, children were swinging on the porch swing
Papaw had made by hand
or chasing one of the neighbor's cats,
or each other.

In the evening, those who remained would
make their way to the back porch
and sit on lawn chairs
or, if they were lucky,
the other swing Papaw had made by hand.
(I claimed partial ownership since

it hung on my old swing set frame.)

I can still hear its squeak;
it was music to our ears.
The best part of the whole experience
was mealtime.
It was a time when we all came together with
one purpose.
It was more than just the food.
It was the togetherness of the moment,
the noise of joy,
the aroma of family.

Uncle Dennis, Aunt Bernice, Uncle Bill,
all the great uncles and aunts,
Mema, Papaw and my dad are all gone now.

That wonderful house with over seventy years of
memories burned to the ground a few years ago.

I miss those moments,
the smells,
the noise,
the feel of love.

I know that one day there will be a
great meal laid before me.
It will be a wonderful reunion.
A celebration.
A great family meal.

I hope God lets Mema do the cooking.

Luke 22:27-30 (MSG)

"Who would you rather be: the one who eats the dinner or the one who serves the dinner? You'd rather eat and be served, right? But I've taken my place among you as the one who serves. And you've stuck with me through thick and thin. Now I confer on you the royal authority my Father conferred on me so you can eat and drink at my table in my kingdom and be strengthened as you take up responsibilities among the congregations of God's people."

I REMEMBER SUMMER

I remember summer days,
When we were young,
At Mema's place.

I remember the summer sun.
We played so hard,
Had so much fun.

I remember summer nights,
Played hide and seek,
And flashlight fights.

I remember the summer moon,
That lit our night,
Ended too soon.

YOUR STORY

Do you remember those days of youth,
at your grandparent's house?

Write your experience;
paint a picture with words and imagery.

What happened?
What did you see, hear, taste?
How did you feel?
What have you learned?

_____

_____

_____

_____

_____

_____

MY FIRST LOVE

In the sixth grade,
I was in love with Darla.
Darla was the most beautiful girl
I had ever seen.

I sat in class and just stared
at the back of her head.
I loved her hair,
her eyes,
her face.
I loved Darla.

One day in physical education class,
we had to stay inside because of rain.

So we did what we always did
on rainy days: square dance.

I often fantasized about one day getting
to hold Darla's hand when we square danced.

My dream came true!

By some miracle, or fate, or luck,
or perhaps the grace of God,
Darla and I were paired as partners.

The moment of ecstasy was soon to be mine.

When it came time to hold hands I felt faint,
took a deep breath and slowly
slipped my hand into her -
cold,
sweaty,

clammy
hand.
My heart sank.

My love for Darla died that day
because of clammy hands.

We all experience disappointments.
We don't want to be disappointed.

We want to be impressed.

We seek to be impressed by tourist attractions,
by the latest gadget,
by fame or fortune.

But all earthly things we seek to "wow" us
will eventually disappoint
or lose their "wow" factor.

If you look below the surface
all people and things will disappoint.
All fall short of true glory.

True glory can't be fulfilled until we come into
the presence of God.

Psalm 29 (NLT)

A psalm of David.

Give honor to the LORD, you angels;
give honor to the LORD for his glory and strength.

Give honor to the LORD for the glory of his name.

Worship the LORD in the splendor of his holiness.

The voice of the LORD echoes above the sea.
The God of glory thunders.
The LORD thunders over the mighty sea.

The voice of the LORD is powerful;
the voice of the LORD is full of majesty.

The voice of the LORD splits the mighty cedars;
the LORD shatters the cedars of Lebanon.

He makes Lebanon's mountains skip like a calf
and Mount Hermon to leap like a young bull.

The voice of the LORD strikes with lightning bolts.

The voice of the LORD makes the desert quake;
the LORD shakes the desert of Kadesh.

The voice of the LORD twists mighty oaks
and strips the forests bare.
In his Temple everyone shouts, "Glory!"

The LORD rules over the floodwaters.
The LORD reigns as king forever.

The LORD gives his people strength.
The LORD blesses them with peace.

LORD I BOW

Words and music by Wes Toller

Lord, I bow before Your throne
Lord, I worship You alone
Lord, I need You now
More than I know how
Lord, I bow before Your throne

Lord, without You I am dust
To have meaning, You're a must
Lord, please take my life
Make all wrong things right
Lord, I bow before Your throne

It's Your blood that has saved me
It's Your grace that sustains me
It's Your constant love that won't give up
When I've given up on me

Lord, I don't know what to do
But to trust and lean on you
When life falls apart
I can feel Your heart
Lord, I bow before Your throne

YOUR STORY

Do you remember your first love?
How your heart felt?

Write about your experience.
What happened to that "love"?

What is God telling you about love?

Where are you in your relationship with God?
Where is God in relationship with you?

What impresses you?
What memories came to your mind as you read?

_____

_____

_____

_____

_____

_____

_____

_____

I WALKED AWAY FROM MY FRIEND

In the summer of '68, my family moved to
Security, Colorado, just south of Colorado Springs.

The first person I met on our street was Butch.

Butch was tall,
big,
strong and
black.

I was little,
skinny,
weak and
white.

We were both trying out for football
during our tenth grade year
and quickly became best friends.

That summer we spent about
every waking moment together.

Butch's Dad was in the military,
had just returned from Vietnam and
was stationed at Fort Carson.
Butch shared a lot about his
feelings during that time.

We went to the same church,
which was not unusual in a military town.

Every day we would spend hours
throwing the football or kicking it to each other,
then running for the touchdown.

I would always get tackled.

Occasionally, Butch would lift me up
over his head as he tackled me,
and then throw me to the ground.

He would always get a touchdown,
usually with me holding on to his leg
and never slowing him down.

We had fun.
The best fun.
Good clean fun.

He was my bodyguard and
we were the best of friends.

School started and we played football.

Butch was good, really good, a natural.

I had heart but not ability,
so I did a lot of cheering from the bench.

Butch was moved to the varsity team
after about three games, and became a star.

He was busy, had new friends and
our friendship disappeared
- slowly.

We moved to another house in town
away from that street with so many memories.

Then, halfway through my junior year,
we moved to Amarillo, Texas.

After graduation,
I moved back to Colorado Springs and
began working for Youth for Christ.

I had heard that Butch had been shot in a robbery.
He was the bad guy.

I went to the base hospital at Fort Carson where
Butch was being treated.

As I was visiting with him,
he told me he didn't need the money,
but someone had dared him to do it -
so he did.

He was shot twice in the leg,
once in the side and
once in the arm.

He said he was stupid and knew better.
He wanted to change and
come back to God.

Just then, some of his "friends"
walked in
and his whole personality changed.

I slowly
made my way
toward
the door to
exit.

As I left,
I looked back into his room.

Our eyes
made contact.

His look was one of lostness,
longing for past days,
as I did.

Those days when life was simpler,
and two boys,
one black and one white,
could enjoy each other's friendship.

Those eyes also said,
"I want to change, but I can't."

I walked away
and never saw Butch again.

2 Timothy 4:4 (MSG)

They'll turn their backs on truth and chase mirages.

BELIEVE

Those who say, "There is no God,"
  Close their life to meaning.
  Too stubborn to open eyes,
  To see God's love beaming.

Those who say, "There is no God,"
  Close their mind to living.
  Too loud to open their ears,
  To hear God's love singing.

Those who say, "There is no God,"
  Close their heart to true peace.
  Too hard from a life unlived,
  To feel God's love increase.

In their dying breath they see,
  Two roads, one less traveled.
  And before them will unfold,
  A life, unlived, unraveled.

YOUR STORY

Do you regret walking away from an opportunity
to help someone?

Who was your best friend as a child or teenager?

Write about your experience.
What happened to that friendship?

What is God telling you about friendship?

What memories came to your mind as you read?
Write it down.

_____

_____

_____

_____

_____

_____

_____

_____

VICTORY

I was a ninth-grader in
Albuquerque, New Mexico.

Our only relatives in Albuquerque
were my dad's uncle and his family.

My second cousins were a little older
than I was and had an uncontrollable sense of
responsibility to socialize me

They involved me in many of their activities.
One of those activities was a youth club.

At the youth club Christmas Dance,
I danced with an attractive girl.

It was the first and last time
I experienced slow dancing.
(And I'm not really sure it could be
officially called dancing.)

Throughout the evening,
I kept noticing a guy off to the side glaring at me.

I became bored,
called my dad to come get me and
left the dance early to go home.

As I left the building,
I found myself surrounded by ten guys,
all bigger than me and all glaring at me,
just like the guy at the dance.

In fact, the glaring guy was now

in front of me and I knew
he intended to beat the living daylights out of me.
Apparently, the pretty girl I danced with was,
at least in his mind, "his girl."

I knew my short life would soon be over.
I didn't want to fight.
I didn't know how to fight.
I was scared.
I was doomed.

Suddenly,
my 18-year-old cousin,
Ken, was at my side.

He knocked one guy to the left,
another to the right.
Then he got in the face of my archrival and
said, "If you want to fight, fight me!"
I suddenly put up my "dukes" and
felt a surge of courage.
I was ready to fight!

I knew my cousin Ken could whip
those nine guys, and
return to pull the tenth one off of me
before I was beaten to death.

They walked off.
And we had Victory!

You plus God is a majority in any fight.
Victory is guaranteed.
Victory is already won.

1 Corinthians 15:57 (NIV)

But thanks be to God! He gives us the victory through our Lord Jesus Christ.

COURAGE

Once, very long ago
When I was just a child
And had so far to go
I walked into the wild

I wandered upon some woods dark
With secrets that remained untold
And in me a spirit sparked
Adventure to unfold

I was the captain of a ship
In waters yet uncharted
Unstopped by any hardship
Into the darkness I darted

With each step, I was aware
Of slightest sound and movement
I made each step with best of care
While moving toward the moment

The goal of mine to reach that place
Where treasure lay awaiting
With purpose firm, set my pace
A sure hero in the making

The mysteries I would behold
Questions answered before asked
I'll have stories to be told
As they ask about the past

I wandered at my pleasure
And as I made my way
I discovered a true treasure
I found that very day

It was not silver or gold
It was not a buried chest
It was the courage to go
Into the wilderness

YOUR STORY

Did you have awkward years growing up?
Did someone try to help you through those years?
Were you ever "rescued"?

Have you ever had a moment when you
experienced true courage?

Write about your experience.
What happened and what did you learn?

What is God telling you about being
victorious in life?

_____

_____

_____

_____

_____

_____

_____

_____

_____

MICHAEL

Michael came a month early.

I began working at the First Baptist Church
in Seymour, Texas, as
Minister of Youth and Recreation
in February, 1978.

After jogging with two friends,
I went to the church gym to shower and
begin my work day.

I got a call from my wife, Kenett, at 7:30.

"It's time," she said with amazing calmness.

I said, "No, it's a month early."

She said, "No, trust me, it's time."

I rushed home,

got her in the car, and
drove the thirty-five mile trip to Olney, Texas.

We made it in about twenty minutes.
(You do the math.)

All the way we were timing labor pains.
They were about two to
three minutes apart.
I told Kenett they were six to
seven minutes apart.
(I lied.)

We met our doctor at the door.
The doctor and I scrubbed up and
soon we were in the delivery room.

In less than an hour our son, Michael, was born.

He was four pounds, fourteen ounces.
They took him immediately out of the room and
another doctor began working with him.

He was having trouble breathing.
They stabilized him and he was in an incubator
for several days.
He was in the hospital for two weeks.

It was a week before I was able to even touch him.
I never felt so distant, yet so close.

The birth of my son was the most
incredible experience of my life.
To hold this new life that God,
my wife and I created together was something
generation after generation had experienced

but I felt as if I were the first.
I wanted everyone to know:
Life is wonderful,
new life is even better.

Michael's lungs were fine but we
soon learned there was a deformity in his feet.

He was born with severe clubfeet.

For the next two years we made trips
almost weekly to the
Scottish Rite Hospital in Dallas for treatment.

The non-evasive treatment
was not working and it was decided that surgery
would be required.

Michael had surgery on both feet at the
tender age of six months.

After the surgery,
he couldn't be picked up and comforted.

I stayed with him all night and discovered the
only way to calm him and keep him from crying
was to put my hand under his neck and pat him.
I did this all night.

It didn't hurt a bit and was
not at all an inconvenience,
it was for my child who was
experiencing more pain
and discomfort at six months than
I had experienced in my entire life.

It worked.

Michael has led a normal life.
Walks and runs.

And except for what we call
chicken-legged calves and
difficulty standing on his toes, he's fine.

We are forever grateful to the fine people at
The Scottish Rite Hospital
in Dallas for helping our child.

We are also grateful to the wonderful
church family
at First Baptist Church, Seymour, Texas,
for their kindness, support and prayers.

This was a time when people
surrounded us with prayer and we were in
constant prayer for our son.

As a result of those prayers,
we did not notice what a
difficult time we were going through.

As we look back, we cannot understand
how we made it other than through the
strength God gave us and
the uplifting prayers from God's People.

He serves the Lord as
Worship Pastor in an Illinois church.
He and his wife, Paula-Beth,
are very talented
and continue to bless the lives they touch.

Proverbs 3:1-4 (NIV)

My son, do not forget my teaching,
but keep my commands in your heart,

for they will prolong your life many years
and bring you prosperity.

Let love and faithfulness never leave you;
bind them around your neck,
write them on the tablet of your heart.

Then you will win favor and a good name
in the sight of God and man.

HOLD ME

Words and Music by Wes Toller

Hold me with Your hands
Love me with Your heart
Tell me with Your gentle voice
You will never depart
Sing to me the song
Of assurance and grace
And one day I will see Your holy face

I want to feel Your hands around me
I want to feel Your love surround me
I want to hear Your voice tell me things
That I need to hear

Sing to me the song
Of assurance and grace
And one day I will see Your holy face

Hold Me © 2006 Wes Toller
Used by permission

YOUR STORY

Has God brought you through an
ordeal similar to what you just read?

Relate how He gave you additional
strength to make it through that experience.

What have you learned?

_____

_____

_____

_____

_____

_____

WORST CASE SCENARIO

The call defined every parent's nightmare.

"Larry, we don't know where Michael is."

Fear gripped my chest like a cold fist
waiting to tear out my heart.

"What do you mean?"
I said, already trembling.

Richard's voice was panicked,
"We've looked everywhere;
no one is left in the stadium.
He knew he was supposed to ride with us.
We are leaving now, he's not here."

"I'm on my way."

The youth of our church had gone
to an "away" football game.
A forty-five minute drive.

Although Michael was a tenth-grader,
he was also very responsible.

I could imagine several
worst-case scenarios - none of them good.

Was he in a fight and
unconscious under the stands?
Was he kidnapped?
Did he run away?
No, that's impossible,
there are no signs.

When I get there,
what do I do?
Search the stadium.
Where is the stadium?
Call the police.
What is their number?
I was in shock and confused.
The dark night,
too many miles,
too many minutes,
too many worse case scenarios.

I prayed for protection for my son and
for God to intervene.

I was more scared than I had ever been.

Thirty minutes into my drive
to the unknown,
my cell phone rang.
My wife's soothing voice:

"Michael is here."

Relief flowed through
every muscle of my body;
I slowed and turned the car around.

"His friend asked him to ride with
his family and told Michael
he had already cleared it with
the Youth Minister, but didn't.
It was simply a lack of communication."

I hung up,
pulled to the side of the road,

thanked God for deliverance and
cried tears of relief and deliverance.

Psalm 18:2 (NIV)

The LORD is my rock, my fortress and my deliverer;
my God is my rock, in whom I take refuge.
He is my shield and the horn of my salvation, my stronghold.

YOUR STORY

Have you ever experienced true terror?

Did you ask for God's intervention?

What happened and
what was God's obvious involvement?

The Short Cut

After two days of meetings,
I needed to get to work early and I was late.

As I rushed out the door,
my wife said the tire on the left rear was low.

"I'll take care of it,"
I growled as I began my journey.

I stopped at the Quick Stop
on Stevenson Drive, and put air in the tire.
As I neared the exit,
I became impatient with the traffic.
I decided to go right instead of left and
wind my way through the
residential area to find a "faster way."

My mind said,
"You know this won't be quicker."

But I went right instead of left and
turned right again onto a street
that seemed well traveled.

On the first block,
a car was pulled to the side of the road,
and a lady was changing a tire.

Cars passed her by and so did I.

Block one: "She's probably almost done."

Block two: "It's dangerous to stop

and help nowadays."

Block three: "I'm late!"
Block four: "This will bother me all day."

Then the scripture reading from just a
few days ago came to mind -
"To the least of these."

I turned around.

As it turned out,
her car kept falling off the jack
every time she attempted
to get the wheel off the ground.

The only way to change the tire
was for her to hold her foot on the brake
while I changed the tire.

After my "good Samaritan" task was complete,
she gave me a quick thank-you and took off.
(Not the great thank-you I deserved!)
I felt pretty good about myself for a few seconds.

Then the truth of the experience
hit me and hit me hard.

I was not sent down this road
to help a person in need to change a tire.
The situation on the road was not to
help a lady in need;
it was to help me.

I thought of my wife's parents
Kenneth and Cleta Nixon.

It has always been in their nature to help people.
Often, I expressed concern to my wife
about the fact that so many have taken advantage
of their serving and helpful nature.

What I failed to recognize was:
they actually enjoyed helping people.
They never viewed their service as a burden.
It was joyful service to the Lord.

I became ashamed that it was not
in my nature to help people.
I had to be convinced.

I decided at that moment,
I didn't want to be in the group asking,
"When did we see you in need and ignore you?"

Matthew 25: 34-46 (NLT)

Then the King will say to those on the right, 'Come, you who are blessed by my Father, inherit the Kingdom prepared for you from the foundation of the world. For I was hungry, and you fed me. I was thirsty, and you gave me a drink. I was a stranger, and you invited me into your home. I was naked, and you gave me clothing. I was sick, and you cared for me. I was in prison, and you visited me.'

"Then these righteous ones will reply, 'Lord, when did we ever see you hungry and feed you? Or thirsty and give you something to drink? Or a stranger and show you hospitality? Or naked and give you clothing? When did we ever see you sick or in prison, and visit you?' And the King will tell them, 'I assure you, when you did it to one of the least of these my brothers and sisters, you were doing it to me!'

"Then the King will turn to those on the left and say, 'Away with you, you cursed ones, into the eternal fire prepared for the Devil and his demons! For I was hungry, and you didn't feed me. I was thirsty, and you didn't give me anything to drink. I was a stranger, and you didn't invite me into your home. I was naked, and you gave me no clothing. was sick and in prison, and you didn't visit me.'

"Then they will reply, 'Lord, when did we ever see you hungry or thirsty or a stranger or naked or sick or in prison, and not help you?' And he will answer, 'I assure you, when you refused to help the least of these my brothers and sisters; you were refusing to help me.' And they will go away into eternal punishment, but the righteous will go into eternal life."

YOUR STORY

How many times have you passed by someone
and felt you should have helped but didn't?

Or did?

Why?
What happened?

_____

_____

_____

_____

_____

_____

_____

_____

THE BEGINNING OF MY ETERNITY

It was the summer of my thirteenth year.

My family had just moved to Olney, Texas.

I had no interest in or
awareness of spiritual things.
My only interests were
entertainment (TV/movies),
food and
play.

I quickly made friends with a few guys
my age on our street.

We played catch, football and watched TV.

Daily, we would walk downtown to the
five and dime store or see a movie.

On the way back we would stop at the Dairy Queen,
where the town pin ball machine
awaited our challenge.

One of these friends invited me to a
hot dog supper and magic show at his church.
I liked hot dogs and magic shows
(two of my three interests).

My dad said on numerous occasions
that the church was full of hypocrites;
I didn't know what hypocrites were,
but I knew what hot dogs were.

How bad could it be if they had a magic show?
Besides, my other friend on the block was
the "evilest" kid I had ever met and
he was going,
so I went with them.

Little did I know that after the
hot dogs and magic show
I would have to stay for
"The Revival Service."

I was upset, so I sat with the "evilest" kid I knew.
He also thought he got more than he bargained for.

We sat on the back pew,
as far as we could get from the preacher.
I felt safe.

During the sermon the preacher told of
his daughter's trust in him.

He said he once stood her on a table top and
asked her to jump into his arms and
without hesitation,
she did.

He said that was the way it was with Jesus.
If I would jump into His arms,
He would catch me and never ever drop me.

I honestly do not remember anything else
he said that night, but those simple words
were powerful and made sense.

The "Invitation" began.

I grabbed the back of the pew in front of me and
held on tight.
I was with the strongest willed kid I knew.
I was still safe.

During the invitation to make a
decision to follow Christ,
the "evilest" kid I knew went forward
to accept Jesus Christ as his savior.

I soon joined him and, as the preacher said,
jumped into Jesus' arms.

My Lord has never dropped me.

Even though I have tried so
hard to squirm out of His arms.

This was the true turning point of my life.

This is the day I began Eternity with God.

Titus 3:5 (NIV)

*he saved us, not because of righteous things we had done, but
because of his mercy. He saved us through the washing of rebirth
and renewal by the Holy Spirit,*

YOUR STORY

Share your experience coming to know
Jesus Christ as your Lord.

How old were you?

What circumstances and influences
led you to that point of decision?
Who helped you?
Who hindered you?

If you have never had this experience
or if you need to refresh your memory of
God's love for you
go to the next page.

THE BEGINNING OF YOUR ETERNITY

Do you have a story about
the beginning of your eternity?
Let's write some history on your life pages!

God loves you like there is no one else to love.
He wants you to experience life to the fullest.

It's all about you!

John 3:16 (NLT)
*For God so loved the world that he gave his only Son, so that
everyone who believes in him will not perish but have eternal life.*

John 10:10 (NLT)
My purpose is to give life in all its fullness.

God cannot look at sin, and
as long as sin dominates our life
He cannot give us what He desires to give.
We work for what we deserve.
God desires to give us a wonderful free gift.

Romans 3:23 (NLT)
For all have sinned; all fall short of God's glorious standard.

Romans 6:23 (NLT)
*For the wages of sin is death, but the free gift of God is eternal life
through Christ Jesus our Lord.*

No matter how we try to live Godly lives,
it is impossible for us to do this without God.

Isaiah 59:2 (NLT)
But there is a problem—your sins have cut you off from God.
Because of your sin, he has turned away and will not listen
anymore.

The God who could not look at sin
found a way to look at me,
a sinful person.

It's all about you!

Romans 5:8 (NLT)
But God showed his great love for us by sending Christ to die for us
while we were still sinners.

God never forces Himself upon us.
Free will is very important to Him.

You have a choice.

Accept the gift He offers
or say, "No."

Romans 10:9 (NLT)
For if you confess with your mouth that Jesus is Lord and believe in
your heart that God raised him from the dead, you will be saved.

There are no secret saints.

Ask Him into your heart now!

Romans 10:13 (NLT)
For "Anyone who calls on the name of the Lord will be saved."

Ephesians 2:8-9 (NLT)
God saved you by his special favor when you believed. And you can't take credit for this; it is a gift from God. Salvation is not a reward for the good things we have done, so none of us can boast about it.

Write the greatest story of all:
The day you met God!

_____

_____

_____

_____

_____

_____

_____

Before you get too far from the previous pages,
I have a few stories and questions for you.

Churchianity

I have served on the staffs of six churches.
All six were very different and all very special.
Each had its own blessings and challenges.
I love church because Christ loved the church.
My love of the church is a result of
my relationship with Christ.
How can it be that some have a love of the church
yet nothing in their life points to a
personal relationship with Christ?

There were two people I encountered
whose situations are
all too common in our churches.

Person one: Henry

Henry was a true chameleon.
He was an upstanding member of the community,
a wealthy businessman and
active in church since birth.
He was a respected and
powerful person in the church,
but was a hateful man to those
who threatened his authority and power.
Church was one of his investments.

One Sunday, the great preacher of the last century,
R. G. Lee, was our guest speaker.

Prior to the worship service, I joined

several deacons, the pastor, and R. G. Lee
in the pastor's office.
Suddenly everyone had left the room and
I was left there to stay with Dr. Lee.

As we sat there, he looked at me and said,
"Do you want to pray?"

I replied with cracked voice, "Yes, sir."

It was a wonderful experience for me to pray with
one of the great preaching giants of the 20th century,
but for my pastor and many others,
the joy of that day was destroyed by Henry.

It was unseasonably hot for April.
The air conditioning was not yet turned on.
Therefore, it became necessary to
open the windows.

Henry threw a fit and verbally attacked the pastor
because he had donated the curtains and
they would surely get dirty if the
windows were opened.

Henry was raised in the church.
Henry loved the church.
Henry, in his words, had a tremendous
amount of money invested in the church.

Henry accepted the church as his savior,
but I saw no evidence he had accepted
Jesus as his Lord and Savior.

Person two: Vince

Vince was in our youth group and was at church
every time we opened the doors.
Vince loved the youth group and loved church.

I discovered Vince was not a Christian,
so I invited him to our house to talk
about his relationship with Christ.

As our conversation began,
he quickly discerned our plan and said bluntly,
"I will NOT become a Christian.
Don't get me wrong, I love church,
I love the youth activities,
but I love other things, too, and
I will not become a Christian."

I wonder if Vince eventually joined the church
to get people to stop pestering him and
at some point someone said,
"Vince loves church and is always faithful;
let's make him a deacon."

I wonder if one day he
will throw a fit and verbally attack a pastor
when he doesn't get his way?

Who are these guys?

Are they you?

Are you following their leadership?

Philippians 2:1-4 (NASB)
*Therefore if there is any encouragement in Christ, if there is any
consolation of love, if there is any fellowship of the Spirit, if any
affection and compassion, make my joy complete by being of the
same mind, maintaining the same love, united in spirit, intent
on one purpose. Do nothing from selfishness or empty conceit, but
with humility of mind regard one another as more important than
yourselves; do not merely look out for your own personal interests,
but also for the interests of others.*

Henry and Vince are like so many in our churches.
They love church but they either don't know Christ
or they are not following Christ.

And guess what?
In many cases they hold the
purse strings or wield power.
And the rest of us follow them by example
in more ways than we care to admit.

The scripture above challenges us to be in unity.
Sadly, most churches are in union, not unity.
Union is being together geographically,
physically in the same area.

Two cats tied by the tail and
thrown over a clothesline have union
but they don't have unity.

These scriptures challenge us
to be intent on one purpose.

Our one purpose is to glorify God.

We are so caught up in our preferences
that we miss our purpose.

We are intent on processes.
We are intent on procedures.
We are intent on protocol.
We are intent on programs.
We are intent on protecting our investment.
We are intent on protecting our preferences.

If we are so intent on these other things,
how can we be intent on our one true purpose?

Here's how we have unity:
Being of the same mind - Christ is Lord!
Maintaining the same love - caring for one another!
United in spirit - following Christ alone!
Intent on one purpose -
glorifying God with our life!

Exciting things can happen in a church and
in you when we have unity.

*My son and his wife wrote the following
as the theme song for our
State Missions Offering a few years ago.*

THE CALL

Words and Music by Michael and Paula-Beth Toller

As He walked upon the earth
He was reaching
And as He set among the people
He was preaching
And all along the road He was teaching to us
By the way he was leading

He gave His time, He gave His all
He gave every part of His life
He gave the call

As I sit in my pew, thinking
The pastor stands before me, preaching
I feel a tug pulling my heart
He is leading

So I'll give my time, I'll give my all
I'll give every part of my life
I'll hear the call

But how will they see
If we don't show
And how will they hear
If we don't go?

So I give my time, I give my all
I give every part of my life
I hear the call

I hear the call
I hear the call
Do you hear the call

The Call © 2006 Michael and Paula-Beth Toller
Used by permission

YOUR STORY

Part 1

I'm sure if you have been in church
any length of time
you've met Henry or Vince.

Have you been caught up in defending
your preferences rather than
asking God for His guidance?

Is your church unified?

Write some stories related to
past experiences in church conflicts.

_____

_____

_____

_____

_____

_____

_____

YOUR STORY
Part 2

Are you a complainer?
Are you and arguer?

Philippians 2:13-14 (NLT)
For God is working in you, giving you the desire to obey him and the power to do what pleases him. In everything you do, stay away from complaining and arguing,

When you complain,
grumble,
murmur,
gripe,
you are either saying
that you are not happy with
God's plan for your life
or
you have rejected His plan and
continue to walk away from that plan.

What is God telling you about
how to respond in the future?

Here's an idea:
Pray about what you don't like.
Ask God for patience and understanding,
and then give your complaints to Him.

Write a prayer to God about
what you have been complaining about.

MY FATHER

On August 30, 1929 in Red Springs, Texas,
a child was born to Oren and Nina Toller.

He was William to his teachers,
Tolly to his family (his middle name was Tolliver)
and Bill to his friends.

When he was three,
his father and mother were divorced.

He would see his father again
only two times throughout the rest of his life.

His mother was still young.
She preferred working and socializing
to raising a child.

So, Tolly was raised by his grandparents,
Cora and Gus Jaco.

Although Gus and Cora were loving,

they had lost control of their children.

The home was a war zone.
There was smoking, drinking,
fierce arguments between family members
and even fist fights.

One day, when Tolly was twelve years old,
he was rummaging through some old papers
he had found in a closet.
As he unfolded a single sheet of paper,
he read words that broke his heart -
"Oren and Nina Toller, having no children,
were granted a divorce."

Tolly felt totally disowned, a non-existent being
in a world of pain and hate.

A year later,
Bill met a person who would
change the direction of his life.
Reverend J. R. Balch, pastor of the
First Baptist Church of Seymour, Texas,
led him to know Jesus as his
personal Lord and Savior.
My earthly father met my heavenly father.

Somehow, he developed a loving,
caring and friendly personality.

He excelled in football and was
offered a football scholarship at a
university in northern Texas.

A few weeks after the semester began,
Tolly was called home.

His grandfather was dying.

He began working to help support his family.

In April of 1952,
Bill married Joan Higgins and
one year and three months later
became a father -
my father.

One month before I was born,
my dad's mother married James Graves
(her fifth or sixth husband), and decided
she now wanted to be a
grandmother and mother.

Even though she had
done nothing to deserve this,
my dad allowed her to have this status.

For the remainder of his life,
my father treated her with respect and love,
and cared for her and her needs.

The love was never properly returned.

On my tenth birthday my grandmother
took all the joy out of the event
with a mean comment.

My dad pulled me on his lap and
comforted me.

My first memory of life itself
was sitting on his lap.

On that day,
he embraced me and said
that ten years ago
I made him the happiest person on earth,
and how very, very special I was.

I would better understand what he was
saying later in life,
when I became a father.

My parents attended church
regularly after I was born.

But something happened -
My father was doing some volunteer work
in the attic of the church.

It was August in Big Springs, Texas.
The only way in and out of that dirty, hot attic
was through the pastor's study.

When my dad came down to get some tools,
the pastor said,
"Hurry up! You're getting my office dirty."

At that moment,
my dad left that church and
all churches.

Even as a three year old,
I can recall my mother asking my father
to go to church.

After a while she only asked occasionally and
eventually even her attendance was sporadic.

My dad would, for several years,
refer to church people as hypocrites.

When I became a Christian at age thirteen,
I came home and shared my experience
with my family and my father's response was,
"Oh, they must have
tricked you into coming forward."

In January of my senior year,
our youth group had a retreat.
My Sunday School teacher shared with me
that many of the men of the church
were very concerned about my dad,
and wanted to visit him.
I warned him that would just make him angry.
But we did pray together -
for my dad.

On the following Monday,
I came home from school and
my mother was crying.
When I asked what was wrong,
she told me that
something had happened to my dad that day and
he would be returning to church with us.

On Wednesday he joined our church,
and on Sunday an all-out effort was
made to get men like my dad to church
to hear him tell his story.

That Sunday he told of
an encounter with a man at work.
In the conversation the man quoted the phrase:
"You're either for God or against Him."

My dad went through the morning with this
scripture echoing through his mind
as he argued with himself:
"I'm not against God!
I'm not for God.
You're either for God or against Him."

Finally, the struggle led him to our pastor and
with our pastor,
he got on his knees,
and my father was reconciled to God.
My father grew as a Christian,
reading and studying his Bible.
He would serve as a:
Sunday School Director in numerous departments,
a teacher, a deacon, a deacon chairman,
lay renewal leader and disaster relief volunteer.

Most of all he was a witness.
He would carry a red droplet,
a game playing piece, in his pocket.
When paying for something
he would bring the change out of his pocket,
always with the red droplet.

Inevitably, the cashier would ask about it.
He would say,
"It reminds me that
Jesus shed his blood for my sins."

He was a witness, to me,
magnifying the power of God
to change a life.

I knew him before.
God changed him.

In July, 1986, at the age of 56,
the Lord called my dad home to heaven.
I don't know why.
I trust the Lord's judgment.

There have been times when
I've achieved something
or something special has happened,
and I think about calling to let him know.

But I can't,
so I ask Jesus to share it with my dad and
tell him I love him.

He was born.
He grew to manhood through adversity and strife.
He fell in love and married.
He raised a loving family.
He completed his life.

He was my father, my friend,
and a witness to me and many others
through a life changed
by the power of the love of God.

2 Corinthians 5:17 (NIV)

Therefore, if anyone is in Christ, he is a new creation; The old has gone, the new has come!

YOUR STORY

Unfortunately, not everyone
has a loving, caring father.

In my life,
I have been doubly blessed:
I had a wonderful relationship
with a loving father and
a wonderful friendship
with a remarkable father-in-law
Both have been loving fathers,
husbands and servants of Christ.

What was your father's history?
What made him who he was?
How did he influence your life?

_____

_____

_____

_____

_____

_____

_____

_____

_____

THE MAGNIFICENT MOTHER

It was my mother
Who brought me into the world
Who cared for me and protected me
Who repaired the scrapes and bruises
even those unseen

It was my mother
Who taught me right from wrong
Who prayed me through my perilous youth
Who had faith God would use me
even when it seemed there was nothing to use

It was my mother
Who laughed at unfunny riddles and jokes
Who always loved and never hesitated to say so
Who knew I could accomplish anything
and gave me willingly to God's perfect plan

It was my mother
Who guided me when life's path divided
Who lived great faith and faithfulness
Who influenced my life
And everyone I touch

*My very talented and sweet daughter-in-law
wrote the following song as a gift to her mother.*

*The music and lyrics are a
wonderful tribute to her mother
and all loving mothers.*

MOMMA'S SONG

By Paula-Beth Toller

I remember the days of pig tails and curls,
of Barbies and Cabbage Patch Kids.

Bein' tucked in at night by the sweet lullabies
as my mother would sing me to sleep.

Those times may be no more,
but one thing is for sure -

You kissed the scrapes,
wiped the tears,
through all the years,
never asked for a thing in return.

You showed me love,
gave me hope,
that one day I would grow
into the woman you knew I could be,
and that's why you mean everything to me.

Lookin' back on the years of my childhood days
I remember one thing more than the rest;
How the faith that you showed
and that love that you gave

led me closer to my Jesus each day.

It may have been long ago,
but I remember it more than you know.

'Cause you kissed the scrapes,
wiped the tears,
through all the years,
never asked for a thing in return.

You showed me love,
gave me hope,
that one day I would grow
into a woman you'd be proud to see,
and that's why you mean everything to me.

And now I can see that everything I am now
is because of all you've been to me.

'Cause you kissed the scrapes,
wiped the tears,
through all the years,
never asked for a thing in return.

You showed me love,
gave me hope,
that one day I would grow
into the woman you knew I could be,
and that's why you mean everything to me.
Yes, that's why you mean everything to me.
My momma' you mean everything to me.

Momma's Song ©2006 Paula-Beth Toller
Used by Permission

I read the following scripture at my
Mother-in-Law's funeral.
(Cleta died in August, 2001.)
It truly described her spirit and
her love for her family.

PROVERBS 31:10-31 (MSG)

A good woman is hard to find,
and worth far more than diamonds.
Her husband trusts her without reserve,
and never has reason to regret it.
Never spiteful, she treats him generously
all her life long.
She shops around for the best yarns and cottons,
and enjoys knitting and sewing.
She's like a trading ship that sails to faraway places
and brings back exotic surprises.
She's up before dawn, preparing breakfast
for her family and organizing her day.
She looks over a field and buys it,
then, with money she's put aside, plants a garden.

First thing in the morning, she dresses for work,
rolls up her sleeves, eager to get started.
She senses the worth of her work,
is in no hurry to call it quits for the day.
She's skilled in the crafts of home and hearth,
diligent in homemaking.
She's quick to assist anyone in need,
reaches out to help the poor.
She doesn't worry about her family when it snows;
their winter clothes are all mended and
ready to wear.
She makes her own clothing,
and dresses in colorful linens and silks.
Her husband is greatly respected
when he deliberates with the city fathers.
She designs gowns and sells them,
brings the sweaters she knits to the dress shops.
Her clothes are well-made and elegant,
and she always faces tomorrow with a smile.
When she speaks she has something
worthwhile to say,
and she always says it kindly.
She keeps an eye on everyone in her household,
and keeps them all busy and productive.
Her children respect and bless her;
her husband joins in with words of praise:
"Many women have done wonderful things,
but you've outclassed them all!"
Charm can mislead and beauty soon fades.
The woman to be admired and praised
is the woman who lives in the Fear-of-GOD.
Give her everything she deserves!
Festoon her life with praises!

YOUR STORY

Equal time.
What about your mother?

Same questions as before:
Unfortunately, not every mother is
kind and loving.
But I think most mothers are and
I believe, although it comes naturally for most,
it also comes as a result of great
sacrifice and selflessness.

Again, in my life,
I have been doubly blessed:
I had a wonderful relationship
with a loving mother and
a wonderful friendship
with a remarkable mother-in-law
Both have been loving mothers,
wives and servants of Christ.

What was your mother's history?

What made her who she was?

How did she influence your life?

HOME

I have lived in fifty-six different
houses in my lifetime.

My dad was a construction worker,
so we moved a lot.
He would get a good job;
we would move into a nice house.
He would get laid off;
we would move to a not-so-nice house.

He used to say that whenever a
U-haul trailer came by our house,
the furniture would start moving toward the door.

Whenever a move occurred,
we always got rid of things
that were broken and things we didn't need.

When I went to a new house
some of the ways I would do things changed.

Things were in a different place.
But I was still the same person.

The ultimate statistic is:
one out of one dies.

Life is terminal.

For the Christian death
is a move from one house into another.

Although we like
the shack

we're in,
we know there is
a mansion waiting for us.

Right now we're renting,
but one day we will inherit the riches of heaven.
In heaven gold is like asphalt.

Heaven is not just a house,
it is
Home.

If you are reading this, you aren't home yet!

John 18:36 (NLT)

Then Jesus answered, "I am not an earthly king. If I were, my followers would have fought when I was arrested by the Jewish leaders. But my Kingdom is not of this world."

THE TREASURE

I opened
a dusty old box
and found a long-lost treasure.
One cherished,
with value unmeasured.

It brought to mind
fond memories
of happy times and joyful acts.
It took me to another time,
an era long forgotten.

How it found its way here?
I do not know.
What brought me here?
I cannot say.

All I can do
is gaze in wonderment,
At a thing
so significantly small.

It lay in darkness
far too long;
now released to renew my mind
with numerous possibilities.

What must I do
with this treasure found?

I placed it back in the box
as carefully as I took it,
in hopes
that one day I'll return
to find a long lost treasure.

YOUR STORY

Do you fear death?
Why or why not?

Where is home to you?

_____

_____

_____

_____

_____

_____

_____

_____

_____

_____

_____

_____

_____

THE SKI LESSON

January 24, 1973, was the day
Dave and I carefully packed to go
snow skiing for the first time.

It was a general assumption
that residency in Colorado
required proficiency in slope jumping.
Neither of us had ever been skiing and
it was embarrassing to answer the question:
"Have you ever been skiing?"

We rented our gear and got a map
for the trip to Breckenridge, Colorado.

We carefully picked a Monday after colleges and
high schools would be back in session.
We wanted to learn how to ski without
worrying about girls laughing at us.

Unfortunately,
former President Lyndon B. Johnson,
showing complete lack of concern for our plight,
had died the previous week and
schools closed on Monday (our Monday)
for his funeral.

This proved to be our misfortune
as the "laughing girls" mourned his loss
on the slopes of Breckenridge.

The first of numerous humiliating experiences
was simply getting up the hill.

The "t-bar" lift is a system for pulling skiers uphill.

A steel rope runs over a series of wheels,
powered by an engine.
Hanging from the rope overhead are
vertical cables attached to a T-shaped bar
that is placed behind the skier (yawn).

I waited in line for my turn and
shuffled into place.

When the t-bar came behind me,
I sat down,
it gave way–
I fell down.

Skis popped off my boots.
Ski poles went flying and
I crawled out of the way.

I gathered my rented equipment and re-suited.
I was determined to get up that hill,
I stood in line again.

My turn came once again;
it was apparent by his expression,
the attendant did not share
the same confidence I had.

The t-bar came around and
I grabbed the cable and pulled,
it pulled with me -
I fell down.

Again, skis popped off,
ski poles went flying and
my pride was demolished.

I went for my third and final approach.
If this didn't work,
I was going to buy rolls of gauze,
wrap up my leg and find a place to
pretend my "good time" was cut short
by an unfortunate accident.

If I couldn't go up the hill without injury,
how did I ever hope to
come down the hill alive?

I got back in line.

When my turn came,
I said to the attendant,
who recognized me immediately,
"How do you do this thing?"

He said, "Just stand there."

"Just stand there?"

"Just stand there.
Don't sit,
don't pull,
just stand there.
It'll take you up the mountain."

So I just stood there and
it took me up the mountain.

Later, as I reflected on this experience,
I thought of my relationship with God.

Sometimes I sit down and say,
"It's your thing, your problem;

let me know if I need to move."
I expect to lay dormant and
God will take care of me–
I fall down.

Other times,
I pull on God.
I say, "You really don't understand the
dynamics of this situation,
Here's how I want you to take care of me" -
I fall down.

But if I stand willing
to go anywhere He wants me to go,
He takes me up
this dangerously wonderful mountain
called life.

I think I'll just stand here.

Romans 8:14

For all who are led by the Spirit of God are the children of God.

ALL THAT YOU WANT ME TO BE

Words and music by Wes Toller

What am I doing here?
What are the answers I seek
For all questions I think?

Why am I standing here?
What is the reason for my life?
Would You make everything clear?

So here I am with an open mind
And a willing heart to receive
I am turning to the one who created me

The reason why I'm asking is
Because I need something that's true

I am asking of You
On bended knee
Make me all that You want me to be

Where do I go from here?
I know there is more to this life
I know there are reasons that I need to hear

Who was I made to be?
Lord, I am drawn to Your presence
You have the answers I seek

I believe that I will find
My purpose my destiny
Surrendering completely Lord at Your feet

So I look up to the One in whom
The questions can be released

I am asking of You
On bended knee
Make me all that You want me to be

I look at the earth and I am so small
The difference I make is no difference at all
Then I look at You Creator and Friend
I was made in Your image, in You I begin

So here I am with an open mind
And a willing heart to receive
I am turning to the One who created me

I believe that I will find
My purpose my destiny

I am asking of You
On bended knee
Make me all that You want me to be

Make me all that You want me to be

Make me all that You want me to be

All That You Want Me To Be © 2006 Wes Toller
Used by permission

YOUR STORY

God teaches us lessons from experiences.

What experiences has God used to teach you something?

_____

_____

_____

_____

_____

_____

_____

_____

_____

_____

_____

MOUNTAIN VIEW

April 2005

As I write this I am attending the
Arkansas Folk Festival in
Mountain View, Arkansas.

This is an event our family has
attended on numerous occasions.

Over twenty thousand people
make the pilgrimage to this tiny, quiet town
to play their musical instruments,
sing or simply enjoy the music.

I have hours of video and numerous photos
to document our experience.

This year, I decided not to bring the video camera.
I wanted to experience this phenomenon
through my eyes rather than through a lens.

As I walk around the courthouse square,

I observe more talent and musical joy
in a square block than one can imagine.

Scattered throughout the square and
overflowing into the adjoining streets,
small groups assemble to play their music.
In most cases they are strangers,
meeting for the first time
while they tune their instruments.

Instruments in the group may include:
a guitar, banjo, bass, fiddle (not violin),
mandolin, and an array of other instruments.
I have even seen a bagpipe.

There is no need for electricity;
all is natural and the music flows all day,
deep into the night.

They have an obvious purpose;
they know why they are here,
and they know what they must do.

What happens next comes as
naturally as breathing.
They come together to play music,
their music,
music from the land and
from living -
Folk music.

As they play, all the folk around are
absorbing the wondrous sound of the music.

It amazes me how natural it is for these musicians
to play this music.

It is not second nature for them.
It is so interwoven into their lives
that the music is part of their being:
it is who they are and where they have been.

They do not practice-
they play and sing music.

They do not seek perfection -
they play and sing music.

They do not seek glory or recognition -
they play and sing music.

The music is a natural expression of
who they are.

They play and sing because
they love the music.

Although I do not play and sing,
I observe,
absorb and enjoy.

The music touches my soul.

I join the others in this pilgrimage and,
although I do not know the
language the music speaks,
I hear it in my dreams and
long for the peace and serenity it gives.

I am privileged simply to listen.
I am honored simply to stand in the
presence of these artists
as they paint the air around me.

Mountain View is,
has been, and
always will be a special part of my life.

What an amazing world this would be
if Christians lived out their Christianity
like Ozark musicians lived out their music.

If being Christian was something
we didn't have to force,
learn,
practice or
discipline ourselves to be.

What if we lived out our Christianity
because it was truly part of
who we are rather than
who we hope to be or
what we felt obligated to do.

What if Christ was truly
interwoven into our lives in such a way that
He was truly part of our being and
those who observed us could see Christ so clearly,
because of our living.

What if we loved God like
Ozark musicians love music?

Matthew 22:35-37 (NIV)
*One of them, an expert in the law, tested him with this question:
"Teacher, which is the greatest commandment in the Law?" Jesus
replied: "Love the Lord you God with all your heart and with all
your soul and with all your mind."*

YOUR STORY

Share an experience
prompted in your mind from this story.

Have you had what you would call a
unique experience from a trip?

_____

_____

_____

_____

_____

_____

_____

_____

MISSING

My sister had been through a divorce and
was living with my parents.
One year after the divorce she simply disappeared.

We had no idea where she was.
No idea if she was alive or dead.
No idea if we would ever see her again.

The next six months were excruciating
for my family, especially my parents.

Then, I received a call from
Los Angeles, California -

My sister's voice saying, "I want to come home."

I called my parents and told them the news,
but told them I didn't know what mental state
my sister was in,
so they may want to wait a few days before
coming to Fort Worth.

I went to the airport, bought a ticket and waited.

We got back to my house
at about 7:30 that morning.

Shortly afterwards,
my parents came through the door.

I had told them to wait, but my words, nor
any words could not have kept them away.

Tears of joy flowed.

No questions asked.
No anger displayed.
No whys.
No wheres.
No whats.

Only joy, celebrating a homecoming.
One who was lost was now found!

In Luke's gospel there is a story of
another prodigal child.

He squandered his inheritance and
ended up feeding pigs.
He became jealous of their living conditions.

He decided to return home as a servant and was
welcomed with celebration and open arms.

We are all prodigal children of God.

We have taken the inheritance of God and
squandered it.

We may not have associated with prostitutes
but we certainly have spent much time,
effort and dollars for some form of
entertainment or pleasure to
fulfill our perceived need for
physical and emotional gratification.

In a sense we have been feeding pigs,
compared to what we should be doing in the
fulfillment of our higher calling
to feed the world the Word of God.

Many of us, like the prodigal son,
have come to the point where
we hunger for the bread of life and
thirst for the living water.

We long to return home to a Father
who cares more for the birds of the field and
the lilies of the valley,
than the world cares about us.

When you turn to Him,
He will run to you with arms outstretched,
embrace you, kiss you,
rejoice with all of heaven and
celebrate your return.

God's invitation at this glorious homecoming is:
"Welcome home!"

Luke 15:21-24 (NIV)

"The son said to him, 'Father, I have sinned against heaven and against you. I am no longer worthy to be called your son.' "But the father said to his servants, 'Quick! Bring the best robe and put it on him. Put a ring on his finger and sandals on his feet. Bring the fattened calf and kill it. Let's have a feast and celebrate. For this son of mine was dead and is alive again; he was lost and is found.' So they began to celebrate."

YOUR STORY

"Missing" is one of the most feared
words in my vocabulary.

Have you experienced
a missing person in your life?

Have you been a prodigal child?

_____

_____

_____

_____

_____

_____

_____

_____

_____

_____

_____

_____

_____

SMALL DECISIONS

Part 1

I was attending a conference at Glen Eyrie Castle
over the Christmas break, 1972.
Leaving late one night
I passed by a girl sitting on the steps and crying.

I passed her by.
God impressed on me, "Go talk to her."

I continued out the door.
"Go talk to her."

I headed for my car.
"Go talk to her."

I turned around, returned to those steps and
sat down beside her.

I don't even remember what

Debbie and I talked about.
We exchanged addresses and phone numbers.

Part 2

A few weeks later I received a call
from Debbie's pastor.
Debbie had told him about me and
he wanted me to come to their church
to lead a Youth-led revival.

In late May, Bobby (my best friend) and I
went to Cheyenne, Wyoming, to lead the revival.

The revival was a great success.
After the closing service on Sunday morning,
we went to the pastor's house for lunch.

The pastor asked me where I was going to college.

(Note: I had been to two colleges thus far and
earned a 1.5 grade point average at one and
dropped out before the semester ended at another.)

I said, "I believe God will teach me
everything I need to know."

He said, "Larry, you need to go to college."

Then he tossed a catalogue from
Oklahoma Baptist University in front of me.

Part 3

I returned home and
in June applied for the fall semester.

The semester started in August.
I had a 1.5 grade point average.
I had no money.
It was a private school (expensive).

I was accepted,
sold my car for the first semester tuition and
bought a bus ticket.

When I got off the bus in Shawnee, Oklahoma,
I was in a town I had never been to before
to attend a school I had never set foot in.
I knew no one within a two-hundred mile radius.

I asked directions to the campus and
began my walk carrying two suitcases.
On the way, a man in a red pick-up truck
gave me a ride to campus
(note: My father-in-law owned a red pickup truck
at this time and I always wondered if
he is the one who gave me a ride to campus that day.)

Part 4

A few months after my arrival,
Jim, a friend from Colorado,
asked me to preach a
children's sermon at his church.

I had never even been in Children's Church,
never wanted to speak in Children's Church.
I didn't have a clue as to
what to say in Children's Church.

I said, "Sure."
As I was waiting to speak,

I noticed a cute young lady
who was one of the workers.
Jim introduced us after the service.

Part 5
Jim and I returned for the evening service.
The cute young lady I had met that morning
was there with a friend and walked toward us.

As I looked at her I said, "Will you marry me?"

She said, "Yes!"

I was, of course, joking.
But we were married a little over a year later and
are still happily married with two children.

Wedding Vows for Larry and Kenett

"I love you, Kenett,
as I love no other.
All that I am and have
I share with you.
I take you to be my wife
in sickness and in health,
through poverty and plenty,

in joy and sorrow,
now and forever."

Part 6

What if I had ignored the nudging of the Lord to
talk to Debbie on those steps?

What if I had ignored the simple advice
to go to college?

What if my pride had prevented me from preaching
the children's sermon?
What if I had not
returned to the church that evening?

My entire life would have taken a different path and
all that I now hold dear may not have been.

Psalm 23:1-3 (NIV)

The LORD is my shepherd, I shall not be in want.
He makes me lie down in green pastures,
he leads me beside quiet waters,
he restores my soul.
He guides me in paths of righteousness
for his name's sake

THE PATH

Misty morning
Sun beams glowing
We travel this path
Some never knowing

The path winds left
Then right again
We continue to travel
Toward the end

Beauty is distracting
Tempting us off the path
Pretty flowers, thorny bushes
Lead us to wrath

Keep on the path
With all your might
No matter how narrow
Go to the Light

Jeremiah 6:16 (NLT)

*"Stop right where you are! Look for the old, godly way, and walk in
it. Travel its path, and you will find rest for your souls . . ."*

YOUR STORY

Our paths take many twists and turns.

God has a plan for our life but
sometimes we get off the path.

How has God directed you?

How did you get where you are?

What are the small decisions you have made
that have had dramatic results?

_____

_____

_____

_____

_____

_____

THE LIGHT OF CHRISTMAS

Part I

I've always had a problem with those impatient folk
who have their Christmas present opening
on Christmas Eve.

When I was a child,
we always had to wait until Christmas Morning

Christmas Eve was the longest night of the year.
It was bad enough, waiting for days,
watching the presents under the tree,
imagining what could be under the wrapping.
What could be that shape,
weigh that much and
fit in that box?

We counted the days and finally it would be soon.

"Soon" took so long.

Trying to go to sleep.
Waking up looking at the clock. 1:00.
Again, 3:24.
Again, 5:30.
So close but I dare not get up; I could ruin it all.
Waiting.
Waiting.
Waiting for the light of Christmas Day.

Then the sound of movement.
In what seemed to be seconds
we tore into the presents.

Part II

Christmas is an exciting time.
It touches our hearts and stirs our emotions.

Christmas is more than tinsel, toys and trees.
Christmas is more than
gifts,
greetings and
goodwill.
Christmas is Immanuel.

IMMANUEL! GOD WITH US!

It is God reaching down to lift me out of sin.

God made a strange entrance
into our world that first Christmas.

It was a humble entrance.
No fanfare,

no reception,
no parade,
no glittering decorations;
No first-class, royal treatment for the King of Kings.
Rags.
Straw.
Silence.
The smell of barnyard animals.

He came among us in a human body.
Our kind of body.
A body that became tired and weary.
A body that needed rest and nourishment.
A body that felt all the emotions and hurts we feel.
Immanuel.

God looked at his creation through our kind of eyes.
Heard with our kind of ears.
Smelled, tasted and felt just like us.

When we say, "I'm hungry."
He says, "I know how you feel."

When we say, "I'm lonely."
He says, "I know how you feel."

When we say, "I hurt."
He says, "I know how you feel."

He identified with us.
Immanuel.

Part III

I remember so vividly the Christmas of 1960.
I was seven.

My dad had just lost his job.
We would have to move out of our house
right after Christmas.

My brother, Stanley, had just died in childbirth
on December 19th.

My mother had returned home from the hospital
just days before Christmas but was in bed
resting and mourning the loss of her baby.

In spite of the darkness
that seemed to engulf my family;
that Christmas seemed so much brighter
than any in my memory.

The colors of the
tree,
toys,
books and
clothes are
so vividly etched on my mind.

Although we did not attend any church at this time,
Christian people gave us Christmas that year,
Bringing a tree, toys, and food.

The darkness of that season of our lives
was dispelled by God's special light
reflected through His special people.

We were given the
most wonderful Christmas gift of all–
Love.
Matthew 1:23 (NLT)

"Look! The virgin will conceive a child! She will give birth to a son, and he will be called Immanuel (meaning, God is with us)."

Luke 2:6-7 (NLT)

And while they were there, the time came for her baby to be born. She gave birth to her first child, a son. She wrapped him snugly in strips of cloth and laid him in a manger, because there was no room for them in the village inn.

TINY CHILD, TINY BABE

Words and Music By Wes Toller

Tiny child, tiny babe
Gift of love to us all
Through the sacrifice made
Born to die, born to save
God so loved the world that He gave
God so loved the world that He gave

In this child so small
Despair became hope
Redemption was born
Angels all up above
Saying "Glory to God"
Bowing shepherds adored
And wrapped up in a manger
God presented salvation to us

Tiny child, tiny babe
Gift of love to us all
Through the sacrifice made
Born to die, born to save
God so loved the world that He gave
God so loved the world that He gave

Hanging wounded and bare
On an old rugged cross
Scorned and despised
Was the dear Lamb of God
Taking my sin
But from death He did rise
And in that promised moment
God presented salvation to us

Tiny child, tiny babe
Gift of love to us all
Through the sacrifice made
Born to die, born to save
God so loved the world that He gave
God so loved the world that He gave

For unto us a child is born
A Son is given, a Son is given

Tiny child, tiny babe
Gift of love to us all
Through the sacrifice made
Born to die, born to save
God so loved the world that He gave
God so loved the world that He gave

CHRISTMAS MEMORIES

Early Christmas Morn
The tree is adorn
With lights all a glowing
Presents overflowing

A delightful sound
Of feet hitting ground
Our eyes watching their eyes
Lighting up with surprise

Parent approval
Frantic removal
A wondrous delight
Wrapping paper in flight

Later we reflect
On a day perfect
And the words we adore
"It's just what I asked for!"

Toys and presents go
Disappear like snow
Memories of this day
Will never fade away

YOUR STORY

Christmas is full of memories!
Christmas = Memories!
And a fitting conclusion to this book.

Can you remember the
anticipation of morning as a child?
Do you remember the sounds,
smells,
noise and
observations of Christmas?
Can you recall the joy and laughter
of your children on Christmas morning?
Can you remember times with family and friends?
Are there also sorrowful times
you have experienced during this season or
a vacancy at the dinner table?

You can write a whole book
about your memories of Christmas!

So Write!

EPILOGUE

HIS STORY
(A Monologue)

When Rembrandt painted the crucifixion,
He portrayed the suffering and anguish of the cross.

He captured the attitudes of the characters around the cross by
their facial expressions.

He painted himself in the crowd.

This was Rembrandts' way of saying,
"I was there, too!
I helped crucify Jesus!"

We, too, were there;
standing with Rembrandt,
in the shadows -

On a rough wooden cross hangs an innocent man.
A man who is being punished for a crime he didn't commit.

The sky is growing dark and
there is an evil all around but it's strange;
there is also good,
overpowering good,
overpowering evil
at the same time.

All heaven
and earth
And hell
are focused in on this moment in time,

this place,
this man.
All time and eternity,
past,
present, and
future
meet on this rocky hill.

Golgotha,

the skull they call it.

We've come to see this man and what he will do.

A light breeze comes from the north.
No, south.
Or is it the west?
I'm not sure.

It's dark,
very dark
but it's mid afternoon.

People are weeping,
laughing,
playing games,
looking to him in horror,
in disbelief.

All people are here.
All people of all time:
Past, present and future are here!

I am here; you are here.

Jesus screams in agony.

I look around to see if anyone notices my guilt.
And so do you.

Many are like us;
we try not to show our emotions,
our guilt.

But we are guilty.
I am and you are.

We both know who should be on that cross
instead of Jesus.

Do you remember last night?
He asked us to stay awake with Him and pray.

We fell asleep.

We were there when they arrested Him.
You grabbed one arm and I grabbed the other
and we led him away.

You ran.
You said you'd never leave Him,
but you ran.

You sat in judgment of Him and condemned Him to death.
You took the whip,
the cat of nine tails, and laid open His back.

His blood poured from the wounds.
You put a crown of thorns on His head and
pressed it down until the blood flowed.

You mocked Him
and beat Him.

You slapped Him
and spit on Him.
You took a stick
and beat him.

He
was
hardly
recognizable.
Not one inch of his body was without a bruise,
a cut,
or some other injury.

You were there and so was I.

We did all this to him and more.

You yelled for Barnabas,
the murderer, to be freed.
Demanded that Jesus be crucified.

You walked with Him to Golgotha.
You laughed.
You cried.
You mocked.
You trembled with fear.

You threw him on to the rough cross
and as I held his arm in place
you took the hammer and
down,
Down,
down it came,
striking the nail,
ripping flesh.

He screamed in agony.
You pretended not to hear,
not to show emotion.
You hid your guilt and so did I.

You gambled for his clothing.

You mocked him.
You laughed.
You cried.
You fell on your knees in disbelief.

Here we are,
you and I.

Its dark,
dark as night,
in the middle of the afternoon.

Evil is here,
but not in control.

There is no wind.
All is very,
very
still.

He yells out!

He forgives me.

He forgives you.

He says it's done!
His job has been completed.

And He dies.

All is very still for a moment.

Time itself seems to stop.

Soon, we all turn to each other and
point our accusing fingers and say,
"You did it."

The truth is:
you did do it!
And so did I.

On the cross Jesus bore the sins
of all people of all time.

The guilt.

The shame.

The punishment.

Adam, Cain, Abraham,
Joseph, Ramses,
Aaron,
Saul, Bathsheba,
Aristotle, Jezebel, Ahab,
Alexander the Great,
Cleopatra, Peter, James,
Barabbas, Judas, Nero,
Augustine,
Genghis Kahn,
Muhammad, Henry the 8th,
Martin Luther,

Rembrandt, George Washington,
Benedict Arnold, Napoleon,
Sam Houston,
John Wilkes Booth, Jesse James,
Calamity Jane, Henry Ford,
Adolph Hitler, Albert Switzer,
Queen Elizabeth, Lee Harvey Oswald,
Mao Tse Tung, Mother Teresa,
Saddam Hussein,
Peter Jennings, Madonna,
you and me.

By going to the cross
Jesus was saying very clearly,
there was nothing in
all God's universe
He would not do to provide
redemption for all who would believe.

If I had been the only human being
on this earth to accept
His forgiveness,
Jesus still would have
had to go to the Cross.

And

If I had been the only human being on this earth to
accept His forgiveness,
Jesus still would have gone to the Cross!

Because He LOVES me!

Three days later -

Luke 24:1-8 (NIV)

On the first day of the week, very early in the morning, the women took the spices they had prepared and went to the tomb. They found the stone rolled away from the tomb, but when they entered, they did not find the body of the Lord Jesus. While they were wondering about this, suddenly two men in clothes that gleamed like lightning stood beside them. In their fright the women bowed down with their faces to the ground, but the men said to them, "Why do you look for the living among the dead? He is not here; he has risen! Remember how he told you, while he was still with you in Galilee: 'The Son of Man must be delivered into the hands of sinful men, be crucified and on the third day be raised again.'" Then they remembered his words.

HIS STORY THROUGH YOU

Why is it we remember some things and forget others?
Could it be that we remember an occasion or event
because it left an impact on us?
If our lives are not impacted,
we tend to forget, don't we?

For just a few moments,
will you follow the advice of the angel and
remember?

_____

_____

_____

_____

_____

_____

TATE PUBLISHING *& Enterprises*

Tate Publishing is commited to excellence in the publishing industry. Our staff of hightly trained professionals, including editors, graphic designers, and marketing personnel, work together to produce the very finest books available. The company reflects the philosophy established by the founders, based on Psalms 68:11,

"THE LORD GAVE THE WORD AND GREAT WAS THE COMPANY OF THOSE WHO PUBLISHED IT."

If you would like further information, please call
1.888.361.9473
or visit our website
www.tatepublishing.com

TATE PUBLISHING *& Enterprises*, LLC
127 E. Trade Center Terrace
Mustang, Oklahoma 73064 USA